The KnowHow Book of Spycraft

ABOUT THIS BOOK

This book is all about keeping secrets. It shows you how to set up secret meeting places and a secret post office and how to disguise your messages and maps. It shows you lots of secret codes and signals.

On the first page you will meet the Black Hat Spy. Watch out for the tricks he plays in *Spy*

Trick – these are things real spies have done.

There are messages in code all through the book. See if you can work them out – you can check your answers on page 46. On the same page there is a list of spy words if you want to know more about the language used by spies.

The KnowHow Book of Spycraft

Falcon Travis and Judy Hindley

Illustrated by Colin King

Designed by John Jamieson

CONTENTS

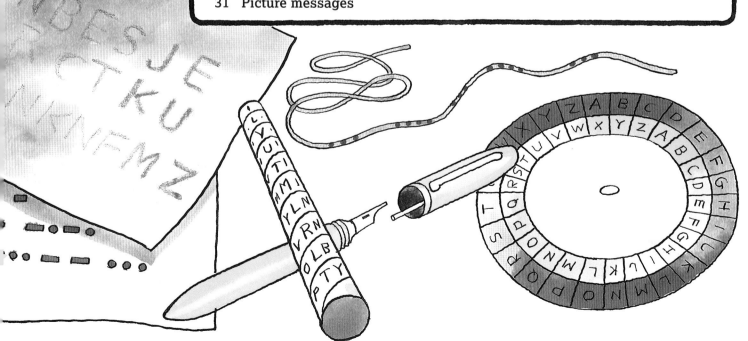

Carrying secret messages

One of the first spy tricks you should learn is how to deliver a secret message. Don't attract your enemy's attention by carrying a bag or holding suspicious-looking papers. With the Stick Scrambler shown below you can encode a message on a paper strip that is easy to hide. See the poster for the methods used by the Black Hat Spy for hiding messages.

Try removing the message with a quick and casual-looking movement – as though you are just hooking your thumb in your pocket or taking a pebble from your shoe. If you hide the message in a pen or hat, you can pretend to leave it somewhere by accident. Then your spy-friend can pick it up later.

On the following pages you will find more details on where to hide your messages and how to pass them secretly to other spies.

Spy language:
A spy-friend is called a 'contact'.
A spy who carries messages is a 'courier'. A spy who holds messages to be picked up is a 'letter-box'.

HIDING PLACES FOR MESSAGES

PINNED BEHIND LAPEL

INSIDE HAT BAND

BETWEEN STRAPS

INSIDE PEN

INSIDE CUFFS

SECRET POCKET BEHIND FLAP

INSIDE SOCK

UNDER FALSE SOLE OF SHOE

BLACK HAT SPY

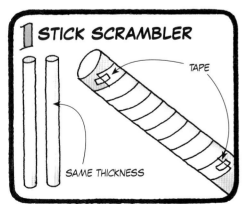

1 STICK SCRAMBLER

TAPE

SAME THICKNESS

Both you and your contact must have sticks of just the same thickness – try pencils. Wind a strip of paper tightly around your stick. Fasten it with sticky tape.

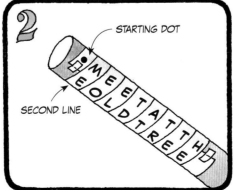

2

STARTING DOT

SECOND LINE

MEET AT THE OLD TREE

Write a message on the strip, like this. Make a dot beside the first letter to show your contact where the message starts. Turn the stick to add more lines.

3

Unwind the paper and the letters will be scrambled up. The message will be hidden until your contact winds the strip around a stick of exactly the same thickness.

1 FALSE SOLE

DRAW AROUND

Place your shoe on a piece of thin cardboard, such as a cereal box. Use a pencil to draw around it.

2

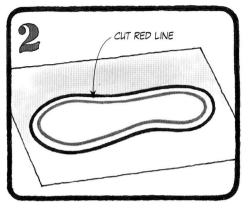

CUT RED LINE

Then, draw a line just inside the outline, like this. Cut this line to make a false sole that will fit inside your shoe.

3

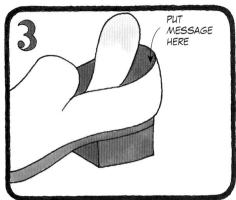

PUT MESSAGE HERE

Slip the message between the real sole and the false sole. Use this method if you think you might be stopped and searched.

1 SECRET POCKET

2

MESSAGE

Cut off the corner of a tea bag and empty out all of the tea. Make two small tabs of sticky tape, like this.

Stick the tea bag in a hidden place, such as the inside of a cap or sleeve. Fold the message very small and tuck it inside.

SPY TRICK

THE SPY IS SEEN STANDING BESIDE THIS WALL. HE SEEMS TO BE INNOCENTLY READING A NEWSPAPER. BUT IS HE?

1 PEN MESSAGE

2

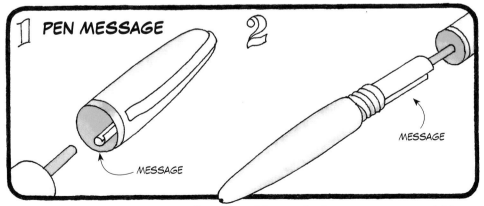

MESSAGE

MESSAGE

Write the message on a small strip of paper. Roll the strip very tightly and keep it hidden in the top of a pen lid.

Alternatively, unscrew a cartridge pen and wind the message strip around the ink cartridge. Then screw the pen together again.

SECRETLY, HE IS HIDING A ROLLED PAPER MESSAGE IN A CRACK IN THE WALL. LATER HIS CONTACT WILL PICK IT UP. TURN THE PAGE TO FIND MORE SPY TRICKS. ⏩

Spy post office

A park is a good place to set up a secret post office. Spies often meet or leave messages in parks because you can wander or dawdle in a park without looking too suspicious. Most parks have open places where you can have a good look around to see if you're being followed. And your meetings with other spies can look very innocent and accidental. Follow the spy in the picture here to see some of the ways a spy post office works.

You can hide your messages in all kinds of places if you make sure your contact knows where to look. But if you bury the message, put it in a small plastic container, such as an empty margarine tub or a plastic bottle. This way it won't get rain-soaked or chewed on by a nosy animal.

A good spy tries not to be seen twice in the same spot. Can you work out how a spy could get to all the message spots in the picture without retracing his steps?

Clue: the letters on the picture spell the name of a car. Put them in order to find the trail.

Spy language: A place where you leave messages is called a 'drop'.

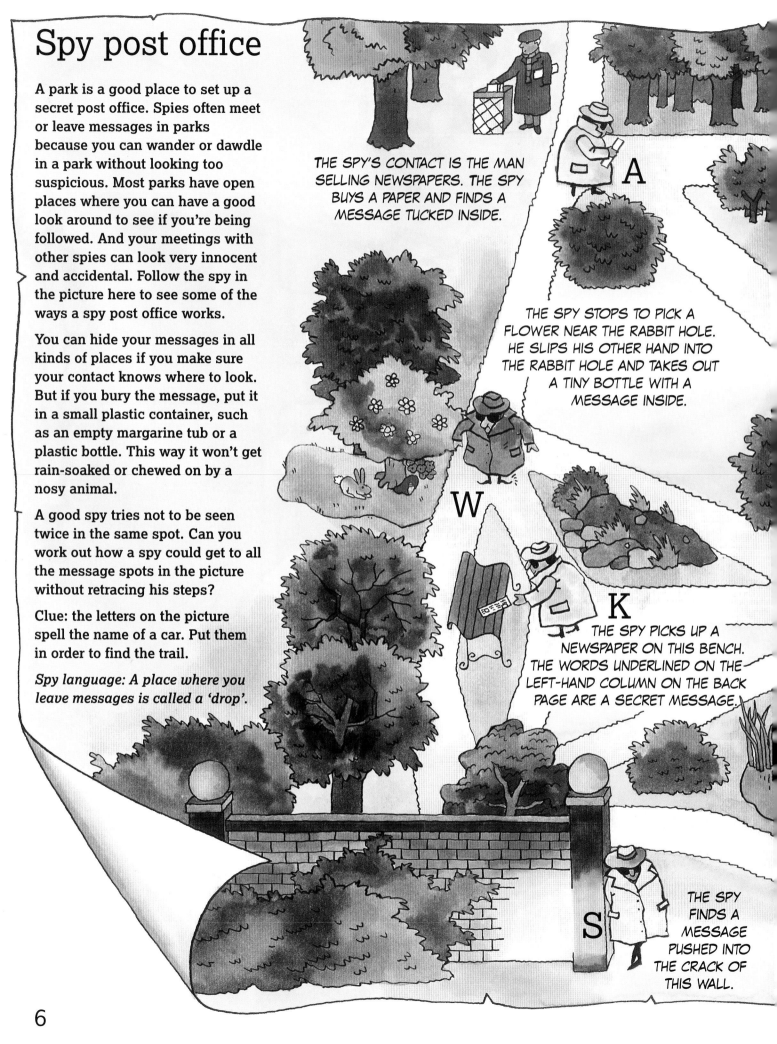

THE SPY'S CONTACT IS THE MAN SELLING NEWSPAPERS. THE SPY BUYS A PAPER AND FINDS A MESSAGE TUCKED INSIDE.

THE SPY STOPS TO PICK A FLOWER NEAR THE RABBIT HOLE. HE SLIPS HIS OTHER HAND INTO THE RABBIT HOLE AND TAKES OUT A TINY BOTTLE WITH A MESSAGE INSIDE.

THE SPY PICKS UP A NEWSPAPER ON THIS BENCH. THE WORDS UNDERLINED ON THE LEFT-HAND COLUMN ON THE BACK PAGE ARE A SECRET MESSAGE.

THE SPY FINDS A MESSAGE PUSHED INTO THE CRACK OF THIS WALL.

WHISPERING WOODS

THE SPY STOPS AND PRETENDS TO SMELL THE FLOWERS. HE FINDS THE MESSAGE IN A SMALL BOTTLE PUSHED INTO THE SOIL.

V

E

G

THE SPY PICKS UP THIS UMBRELLA AND TAKES IT HOME. WHEN HE IS ALONE HE UNSCREWS THE HANDLE AND FINDS A MESSAGE INSIDE.

THE SPY KNEELS BY THIS TREE AND PRETENDS TO TIE HIS SHOELACE. HE FINDS THE MESSAGE UNDERNEATH A TREE ROOT.

L

N

THE SPY SITS DOWN ON THIS BENCH AND FINDS A MESSAGE STUCK UNDER THE BENCH WITH STICKY TAPE.

THE SPY PRETENDS TO STUMBLE AGAINST THIS LOG. HE STOOPS TO RUB HIS SHIN AND PULLS OUT A MESSAGE FROM BENEATH THE LOG.

O

HERE THE SPY MEETS A MAN WALKING A DOG. THE SPY SCRATCHES THE DOG'S HEAD AND FINDS A MESSAGE UNDER THE DOG'S COLLAR.

Colour codes

Suppose you are expecting a visit from your contact when you are suddenly called away on spy business. If you and your contact have a colour code, you can leave a secret message for him or her by putting things with certain colours in your window – or even on your washing line. The picture to the right shows several ways to signal with a colour code. Make sure your contact knows which one you use.

To make a simple colour code, agree with your contact that the position of one colour in a group will have a special meaning. The washing line signal shown on the right is an example of a colour-position code. It can have three meanings, depending on the position of the red socks.

You can also set up a code in which each pattern of colours has a meaning. With three colours you can make six patterns and send six messages. This kind of code is used to make the flower pot signal at the bottom of the page. You can use the sample messages or invent your own messages.

WASHING LINE SIGNAL (SEE BELOW)

SPY WAITING FOR 'ALL CLEAR'

1 WASHING LINE SIGNAL

Red on the left of the group means, 'Danger! Go away!'

2

Red in the middle means, 'We have a message for you.'

FLOWER POT SIGNAL

In this group of flowers the order of colours from left to right can have a special meaning. Here are some examples:

Yellow-blue-red means, 'We have nothing for you today.'
Yellow-red-blue means, 'Meet me at the hideout.'

Red-blue-yellow means, 'All clear – come in.'
Red-yellow-blue means, 'Come back later.'

8

LAMP SIGNAL
RED ON THE RIGHT MEANS DANGER. RED ON THE LEFT MEANS 'ALL CLEAR'.

FLAG SIGNAL
NOT VERY SECRET USED FOR EMERGENCIES

FLOWER SIGNAL
(SEE BELOW)

DOLL SIGNAL
THIS CODE WAS USED BY A FAMOUS SPY WHO OWNED A TOY SHOP. THE WAY IT WORKS IS LIKE THE WASHING LINE CODE. THE RED DOLL IS THE KEY.

Red on the right means, 'Come back later.'

Blue-yellow-red means, 'Danger! Use Plan Z.'
Blue-red-yellow means, 'Danger! Leave area!'

COLOUR DOT CODE

Three colours give you six patterns.

Four colours give you 24 patterns.

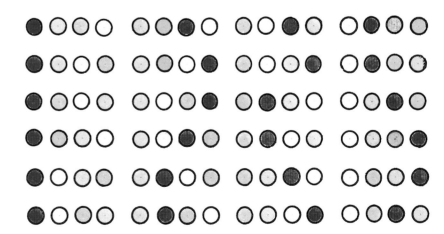

If you use a code with as many as 24 meanings, you and your contact should each have a code book. Use a small notebook and make patterns of colour dots like those above. Write the meaning next to each pattern.

You can put the dots in the corner of an ordinary letter to send your contact a secret message. If you make them look like triangles or flowers, anyone who finds the letter will think they are just decoration.

Clock shop code

The clock shop shown at the far right is a meeting place for members of the QZ Spy Ring. A spycatcher has discovered that the QZ spies are sending messages with clocks and watches. He has just decoded the message spelled out by the watches in the tray at right. Can you use the decoded message as a key to break the code in the clock shop window?

BREAKING THE CODE

The angle of the hands on each watch stands for a certain letter of the alphabet. Copy the watches and print one letter of the watch message under each. Now use this key to decode the message in the window. For example, the hands of the first clock in the window are at five past three. The watch that shows the same time stands for W, so the first letter of the window message must be W.

Warning:
A watch or clock that says 6:30 is a null. A null has no meaning – it is there to confuse the enemy.

Spy language:
A message that is not written in a code is said to be in plain language.

BREAKING THE CODE

The clock code is the same as the flag code called semaphore. The pictures below show how to make the letter U as a flag signal or a clock signal. You will find the whole semaphore alphabet on page 43.

FLAG POSITION

CLOCK HAND POSITION

WATCH TRAY MESSAGE

Victor was arrested last night

This picture shows the tray of watches found by the spycatcher and the message he worked out.

SPY RING

THE **SPY** GETS ORDERS BROUGHT BY...

THE **COURIER**. THE COURIER GETS THE ORDERS FROM...

CLOCK SHOP MESSAGE

The clocks in this window spell out a message. Can you work it out? The clues are in the watch tray.

THE **MASTER SPY.**
THE MASTER SPY IS THE CHIEF OF THE SPY RING. HE MAY CONTROL MORE THAN ONE...

COURIER. BUT THE COURIER ONLY KNOWS THE MASTER SPY AND ONE...

SPY. AND THE SPY ONLY KNOWS THE COURIER. IF HE IS CAUGHT, HE CANNOT BETRAY THE MASTER SPY.

Quick codes

You can make quick, easy codes by making a few small changes in your messages. The best example is the word-split code. Just split the words in different places to make the message look completely different. For example, 'We trail spies' can be changed to 'Wet rails pies' – all the letters are the same, only the spacing between the letters has changed.

You can make other good codes by changing around the message letters in simple ways or adding dummy letters to the message.

On the right you will find examples of these codes and clues on how to break each kind of code.

FIND THE MASTER SPY

The people you see in the picture below are QZ spies. Each has a message for you in one of the six codes shown on the right. Begin with the message at START – each decoded message will lead you to another contact. Break all the codes to find which of your contacts was actually the master spy of the QZ Spy Ring.

BREAKING THE CODES

Try these methods to work out which code was used.
1 Join the first code word to one or two letters of the second word.
2+3 Spell the first few code words, or the whole sentence, backwards.
4 Take away the first letter of each code word and see if the remaining letters make words.
5 Take away the last letter of each code word and see if the remaining letters make words.
6 Exchange the last letter of each word with the first letter of the next.

1 WORD-SPLIT

To break the code, join the letters in a different way.

2 BACKWARDS WORDS

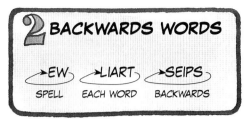

To break the code, spell each code word backwards.

3 BACKWARDS SENTENCES

To break the code, spell the sentence backwards.

4 DUMMY FIRST LETTER

To break the code, cross out the first letter of each word. Make words from the remaining letters.

5 DUMMY LAST LETTER

To break the code, cross out the last letter of each word. Join up the remaining letters into words.

6 EXCHANGED LETTERS

To break the code, exchange the last letter of each word with the first letter of the next.

Mystery codes

The mysterious papers Black Hat is examining are coded messages. These pages show the key to each of them. Can you decode them?

MUSIC CODE

The key to the music code is on the right. It shows which note stands for each letter of the alphabet and for each of the numbers from one to nine. Use 0 for zero.

Match Black Hat's message notes with those in the key, to find the letter that each note stands for. (The first letter of the message is W.)

A dot marks the end of a word.

1 PIG-PEN CODE

This mysterious-looking code is very easy to use. To make the key, first draw the patterns shown here.

1 RAILFENCE CODE

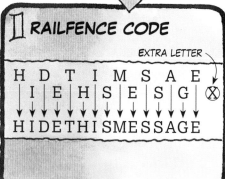

To encode a message, first write the letters in an up-and-down pattern, on two lines. Add a null (extra letter) if needed to make both lines the same length.

2

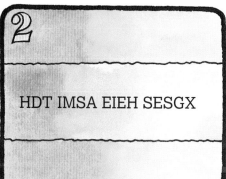

HDT IMSA EIEH SESGX

Now write out the letters of the first line, then the letters of the second line. Put them in groups, to look like words. Make sure your contact knows how to decode this.

3

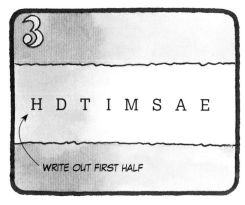

H D T I M S A E

WRITE OUT FIRST HALF

To decode a railfence message, first count out the first half of the message. Write it out with big spaces in between each of the letters.

14

KEY TO MUSIC CODE

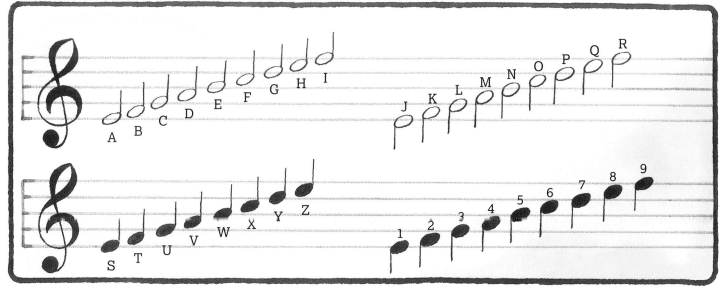

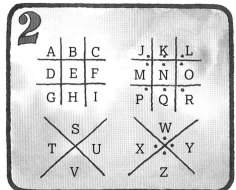

Now write in the letters of the alphabet like this. The pattern of lines, or of lines and dots next to each letter, is used to stand for that letter.

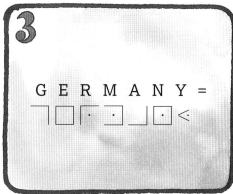

This example shows how the password 'Germany' looks in pig-pen. Now see if you can work out the secret message Black Hat has found.

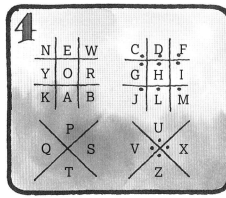

For a more secret pig-pen key, write the alphabet in a different order. Start with a keyword (a word with all-different letters), then add the rest of the alphabet.

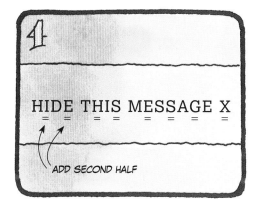

Now put the letters of the second half one by one into the spaces, like this. Try this method on the secret message that Black Hat is looking at.

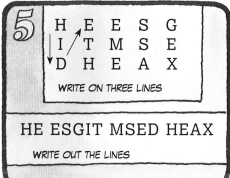

To change the code, write the letters in an up-and-down pattern on three lines, like this. Then write out the letters from each line, as before.

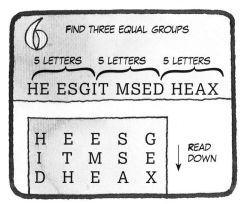

To decode the message your contact must count out three equal groups of letters and write them in three lines again. Then he or she can read down each group of three.

Code machines

With these machines you can encode and decode messages very quickly. The code strip shown below is easy to make. Use it to match the plain alphabet with a code alphabet that starts and finishes at a different letter. For example, start the code alphabet at B. Then change each plain letter for the one that follows it in the alphabet. Change the Zs to As.

To make a code wheel, trace the pattern on page 17. Trace it carefully so that the alphabets line up when you spin the dial.

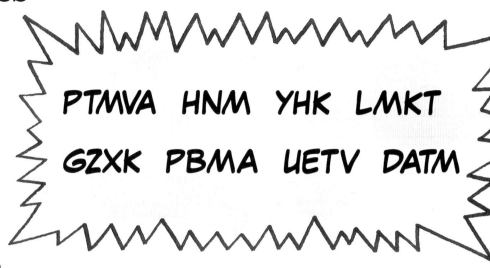

PTMVA HNM YHK LMKT

GZXK PBMA UETV DATM

This message is written in Code T. Match A with T on a code machine to break the code.

When you send messages, be sure your contact knows which code alphabet you have used.

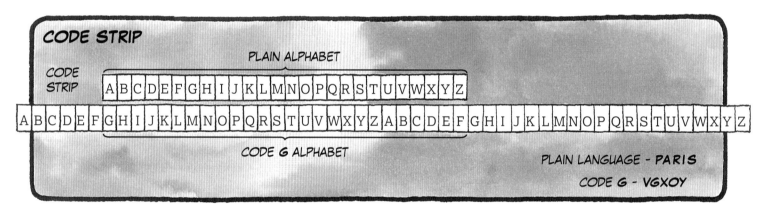

CODE STRIP

CODE STRIP

PLAIN ALPHABET

A B C D E F G H I J K L M N O P Q R S T U V W X Y Z

A B C D E F G H I J K L M N O P Q R S T U V W X Y Z A B C D E F G H I J K L M N O P Q R S T U V W X Y Z

CODE G ALPHABET

PLAIN LANGUAGE - PARIS

CODE G - VGXOY

Mark a strip of paper into 26 spaces, 1cm (½in) wide. Write the alphabet neatly in the spaces. Then mark 52 spaces, 1cm/½in wide, on a strip twice as long.

Write the alphabet twice in the long strip, as above. Slide the short strip over the long strip to line up the plain alphabet with a code alphabet.

For example, slide the short strip so that A stands over G to make Code G. Then match each plain letter with the letter beneath it on the code strip.

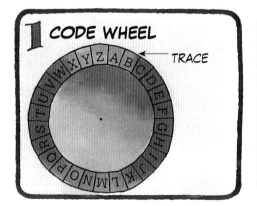

Trace the red wheel from the pattern on page 17. Trace the lines very carefully and mark a dot in the middle of the wheel.

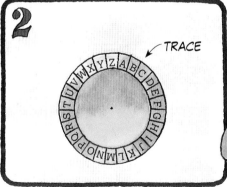

Trace the blue wheel in the same way. Print one letter of the alphabet in each border space, on both wheels. Cut out the wheels.

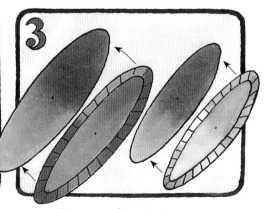

Draw and cut out some cardboard (such as a cereal box) and glue each paper wheel to a cardboard wheel.

TOP SECRET

This is how to use two code alphabets. First print the message. Then print the names of the alphabets over and over to mark each plain letter. Set the code strip or wheel at P and encode all the letters marked P. Set it at Q to encode the rest. Tell your contact to decode with PQ.

	PQP	QPQPQ	PQP	QPQPQ	PQP
MESSAGE	WHO	WEARS	THE	BLACK	HAT
CODE P	L D	T G	I T	A R	W I
CODE Q	X	M Q I	X	R Q A	Q
CODE PQ	LXD	MTQGI	IXT	RAQRA	WQI

CODE WHEEL PATTERN

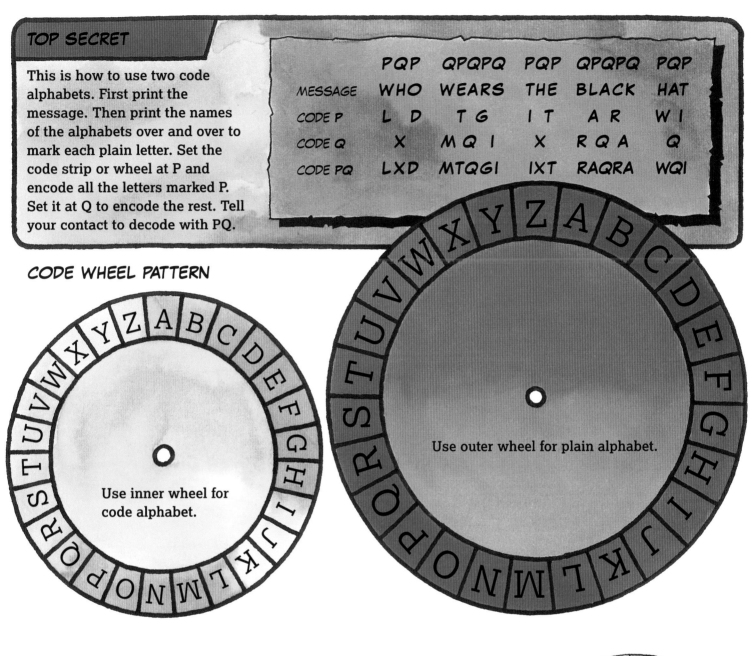

Use inner wheel for code alphabet.

Use outer wheel for plain alphabet.

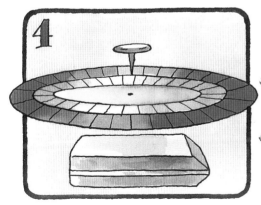

4 Push a drawing pin or thumbtack through the middle dot of both wheels and into a small hard eraser.

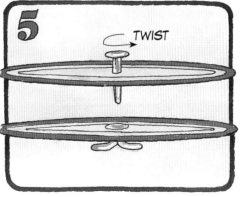

5 TWIST

Alternatively, push a paper fastener through both middle dots. Twist it once to make a hole. Bend out the tabs.

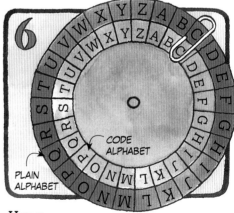

6 CODE ALPHABET

PLAIN ALPHABET

Use a paperclip to hold the wheels in place while you match the plain alphabet with a code alphabet.

More code machines

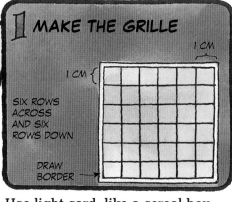

USE A CODE GRILLE TO REVEAL THE HIDDEN MESSAGE.

① MAKE THE GRILLE

1 CM

1 CM {

SIX ROWS ACROSS AND SIX ROWS DOWN

DRAW BORDER →

Use light card, like a cereal box, and draw a square like this. Draw lines about 1cm (½in) apart, as shown, and draw a border round the square. Cut round the border.

1 ENCODING A MESSAGE

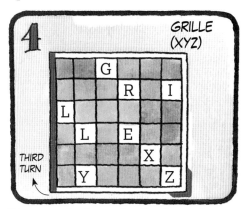

THIS IS HOW

MARK CORNER

Place the grille on some paper. Draw round one corner of the grille to mark its place. Print one letter of the message in each space as shown.

2

FIRST TURN

TO USE THE S-

Now give the grille one turn clockwise so that the top edge becomes the right side. Match a corner with the corner mark. Fill the spaces with letters.

3

-ECRET CODE

SECOND TURN

Give another clockwise turn so that the top edge becomes the bottom edge. Match the corner with the corner mark and fill the spaces with letters.

4

GRILLE (XYZ)

THIRD TURN

Turn again to make the top edge become the left side. Fill the rest of the spaces with letters. Add extra letters if needed to fill all the spaces.

5

```
T E G T O C
H U I R R I
L E S T E S
C L I E S T
H H E O X D
O Y E S W Z
```

When you lift the grille the message will look like this. Write it in a line, like this: Tegtoc huirri lestes cliest hheoxd oyeswz.

DECODING A MESSAGE

First print the message in squares that match the grille. Place the grille over the message with the coloured edge at the top. Turn it to show all the letters.

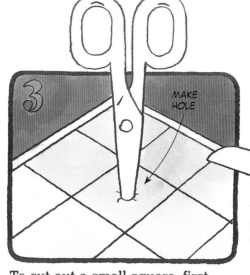

Cut out the squares marked with an x. Colour the top edge. Make an exact copy of the grille for your contact.

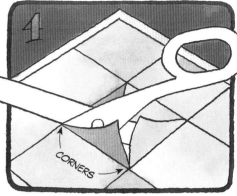

To cut out a small square, first push the tip of your scissors through the centre of the square, as shown.

Then make snips from the centre to the corners, like this. Fold back the four triangles and cut them off.

Here is a different pattern. Hold the grille as shown to begin. For the second step give two clockwise turns so the top edge is at the bottom.

For the third step turn the grille over. For the fourth step give two clockwise turns again, so that the top edge is at the bottom.

SUPER CODE GRILLE

Trace this pattern to make a 144-letter code grille. With this code machine you can write a secret message almost as fast as an ordinary letter.

Black Hat's spy equipment...

Here is Black Hat in his attic den, surrounded by equipment. (You may recognize many of his tools – other pages in the book show you how to make them.) Black Hat has just noticed someone climbing towards the attic on a ladder. It may be the window-cleaner – but it may be a spycatcher in disguise.

In the next few minutes Black Hat must find a way to hide all the evidence that he is a spy. How can he do it?

On the next page you can see how the spy den will look in just five minutes. Can you figure out any of the tricks Black Hat uses to hide everything? The answers are on page 21, upside-down.

AERIAL

TUNER

THE SPY DOES NOT KNOW HIS ROOM IS 'BUGGED'

SHORT WAVE RADIO FOR SENDING SPY MESSAGES

PEN BARREL TWO LENSES

MICRODOT READER - THE TWO LENSES IN THE BARREL OF THE PEN CAN MAGNIFY THE DOT 200 TIMES.

MICRODOT - MAGNIFIED 200 TIMES TO SEE SECRET MESSAGE

CODE WHEEL

BOTTLE OF INVISIBLE INK

HOLLOW RING WITH MINIATURE TAPE RECORDER

SPY MAPS

CODE BOOK - LIKE A FOREIGN DICTIONARY, WITH A SIGN OR NUMBER FOR EACH WORD OR MESSAGE THE SPIES MIGHT WANT TO SEND. VERY TINY.

...and how he hides it away

5 MINUTES LATER

Where is Black Hat's spy equipment now? Turn the page upside-down to check your answers.

Bottle of invisible ink – inside teapot spout.

Microdot – on the side of the envelope that is turned down. A microdot has a shine that a spycatcher might notice.

Microdot reader in pen barrel – put together as pen.

Code book – hidden in teapot inside small plastic bag with elastic band around it.

Hollow ring – on Black Hat's finger.

Radio – behind sliding panel disguised as bookshelf. The books at the end are real. Those on the right are pieces of book-cover stuck to the panel.

Code wheel – hidden under lid of sugar bowl.

Binoculars – underneath the teapot cover.

Maps – pushed into sleeves of coat, which are tucked into pockets to keep maps from sliding out.

Spy maps

Spy maps have to be disguised in case the enemy gets hold of them. These pages show how to disguise a map to look like part of a picture – and how to leave clues to help your contact find the hidden map.

You may want to make a map to show your contact how to get to a new hiding place or 'drop'. On the right you will see how to make a map like this. Be sure to start the route at a place you both know. Tell your contact what the starting point is, and tell him or her the meaning of any map signs you use.

LANDMARKS

A landmark is something along the route that your contact can look for to make sure he or she has come the right way. It could be any odd or noticeable thing, such as a tree with a funny shape or a very tall building or a church. Don't use a car for a landmark – it might be driven away. Use things that will stay pretty much the same. Where your route goes across a park or field, try to show a landmark to guide your contact.

MAPPING A ROUTE

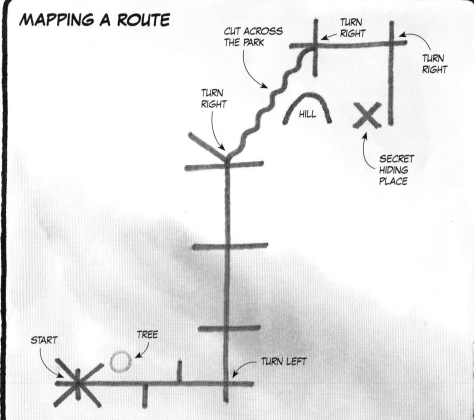

Mark the start with a big X and show a landmark to make clear what direction to follow. Then show every turn you make from start to finish. Mark all the roads that meet your road before you need to turn. If there are none, show a landmark near the turn.

Use a wavy line for short cuts across grass or fields and show a landmark for your contact to walk towards. The marks on this map all have labels. Tell your contact what your marks mean – don't write on the map. Mark a small x at the finish.

SPY TRICK

POSING AS A BUTTERFLY HUNTER BLACK HAT CAME TO A VILLAGE NEAR THE ENEMY CAMP. HE SAID HE'D COME TO PAINT BUTTERFLIES.

EVERY DAY HE WENT OUT INTO THE COUNTRY WITH PAINTS AND A NET. SECRETLY HE WAS PAINTING MAPS OF THE ENEMY CAMP.

IN SPY LANGUAGE, THIS KIND OF MAKE-BELIEVE IS CALLED A COVER. IT COVERS UP THE SPY'S TRUE INTERESTS.

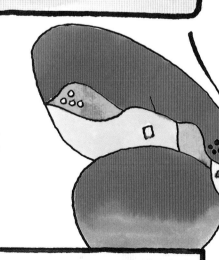

THIS IS ONE OF THE PICTURES BLACK HAT MADE WHILE HE WAS OUT NEAR THE ENEMY CAMP.

DISGUISING YOUR MAP

REAL MAP

MIRROR COPY OF MAP

To disguise the map, first draw a mirror copy of the map next to the real one. Prop a mirror so that it reflects the map and copy what you see. Don't copy the x's at the start and finish. These are clues that mark the real map.

Now draw around the double map to disguise it as a picture. Be careful not to cover up the map. Don't let any picture lines join the lines of the real map or your contact might think they are part of the route.

SPY PRACTICE

Spies have to hurry when they make maps in case the enemy is watching. They have to see all the important things at a glance. Are you good at noticing things quickly? Try this exercise for practice.

Stand outside with a pencil and a pad of paper. Look down the road for about a minute. Then turn your back and try to answer the questions below.

1. Is there a landmark nearby, such as a very tall or peculiar building or hill?

2. How many crossroads could you see?

3. Are there any places that could be used as 'drops'? Remember – pages 6 and 7 show the kinds of places you can use as 'drops'.

4. Are there any parked cars or other places where a spy might be hiding to keep a look-out?

5. Are there places you could hide if you were being followed?

WHEN THE ENEMY STOPPED HIM, THIS PICTURE PROVED HE WAS JUST A BUTTERFLY HUNTER.

BUT...

...THE MARKS ON THE BUTTERFLY'S RIGHT WING WERE REALLY A MAP SHOWING TARGETS TO BE BOMBED. THE LABELS HERE SHOW WHAT THE MARKINGS STOOD FOR.

ACK-ACK GUNS

ACK-ACK GUNS

SIGNAL POST ON HILL

THE LINES SHOW ROADS AND PATHS THAT CAN BE SEEN FROM A DISTANCE.

AMMUNITION DUMP

Spytrap

GAME FOR TWO PLAYERS

Each player has two counters (two spies or two enemy agents). The object is for the spies to reach safety before being trapped by the enemy agents. If one spy reaches safety and the other is trapped, the game is a draw. A spy always starts.

The rules are:
1. A player moves either of his or her counters in a turn. He or she may move any numbers of squares and in any direction, but only in a straight line.
2. If a counter ends its move on a square in a direct line with an

SPY START

SAFETY

ENEMY AGENT START

opponent's counter, the mover says, 'You're covered!' and his or her opponent must move out of the line of fire.

3 If the counter can't move out of the line of fire it must go back to its starting place.

4 An enemy agent can leave its starting place on its next move.

5 A spy must wait at its starting place until it is rescued by the other spy.

6 The other spy rescues it by moving into the line between the two spy starting places.

7 Counters may not pass.

8 A counter may not move onto a square where it is in line of fire from two directions.

9 A safety square can hold only one spy and never an enemy agent.

10 A counter may only move one square at a time in red zones.

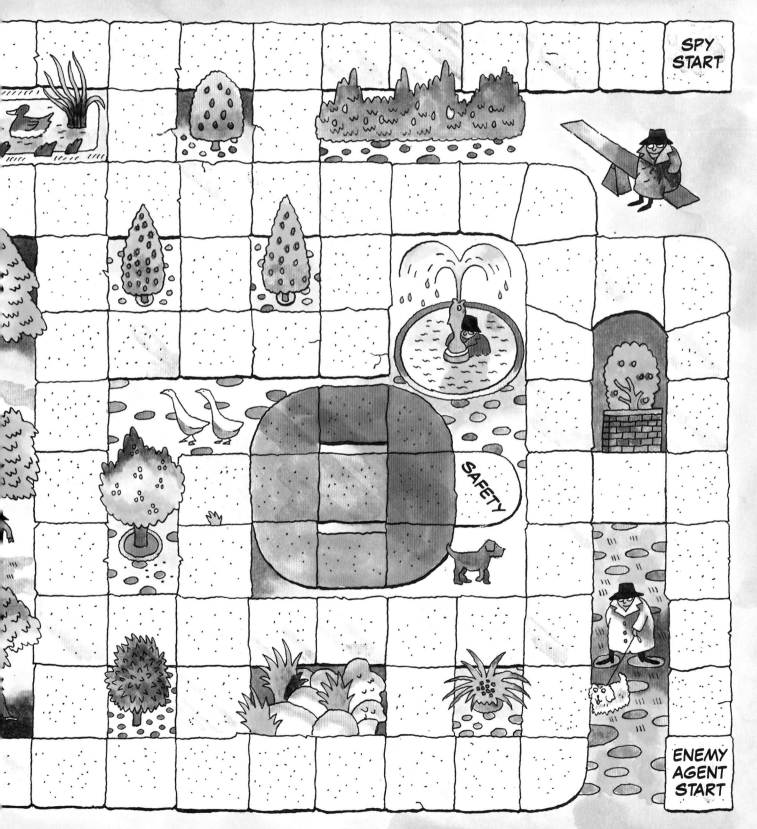

SPY START

SAFETY

ENEMY AGENT START

Invisible writing

A message in secret ink is usually written on the back of an ordinary letter or in the blank spaces between the lines and along the sides.

You will need:

- a piece of white candle
- fine powder for wax writing – you can use powdered instant coffee, chalk scrapings or even fine soil in an emergency
- ink or paint and a brush or sponge to make the water message appear
- a potato for the potato ink well
- some paper – use thin paper for the water mark
- a toothpick

Always mark the message to show your contact how to develop it (make it appear).

Marks to use are:

wx for a wax message
wm for a water message
h for a message that must be heated
x on the message side of the paper

SIGN FOR WAX MESSAGE

Know How
Spycatcher Club
Box WX 123

Dear Member,
To send a really secret message, use invisible writing and a code. Can you decode the password written between these lines? (Pig-pen code, page 14)

Red chalk dust was used to make it appear. Notice the fake address – the letters WX are really a sign that the true message was written with wax.

1 POTATO INKWELL

Hold the potato like this and cut off both ends with a table knife, as shown.

2

Stand the potato on one end. Scoop a hole in the top with a spoon.

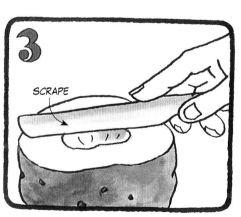

SCRAPE

Now use the blade of the table knife to scrape and squeeze juice from the cut top of the potato into the hole.

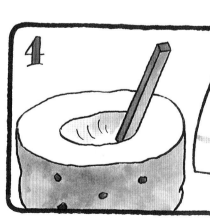

4

Dip a toothpick into the potato ink to write the message. When the 'ink' dries, the message will be invisible.

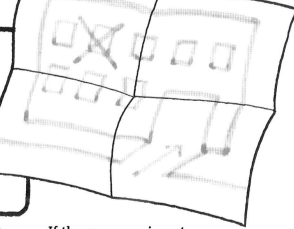

If the message is put in a warm oven (250°F, 120°C, gas mark ½) it will look like this. Make other 'inks' with lemon juice, milk, onion juice or cola.

1 WATER WRITING

DRY PAPER
WRITE FIRMLY
WET PAPER

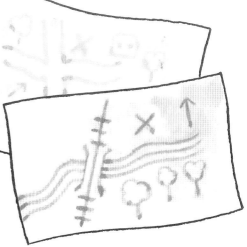

Wet some paper thoroughly. Lay it on a smooth, hard surface. Cover it with dry paper and write firmly. The message will appear on the wet paper when held to the light.

The message will vanish when the paper dries and reappear whenever it's wet. Your contact can brush it with watery ink or paint to make it permanent.

You can make watermark messages on dry paper with a toothpick dipped in slightly soapy water. The soapy shine will help you see what you're doing.

1 WAX WRITING

PAPER WITH WAXED UNDERSIDE
WRITE FIRMLY
PLAIN PAPER

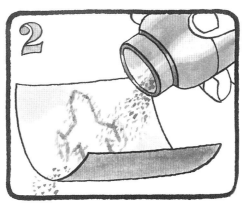

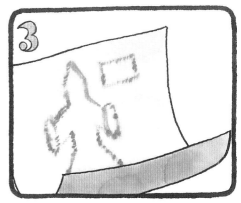

Wax some paper by rubbing it with a white candle. Lay the waxed side on plain paper. Write firmly to print the message in wax on the paper.

Your contact should sprinkle the message paper with powdered instant coffee or chalk scrapings.

When he or she gives the paper a gentle shake, the powder will stick to the message and slide off the rest of the paper.

SPY TRICK

BLACK HAT HAD JUST ARRIVED AT THE AIRPORT. HE WAS STOPPED AND SEARCHED, BUT WAS FOUND TO BE CARRYING ONLY... A SEWING KIT...

THE SPY WAS ALLOWED TO GO. AFTER ALL, A FEW NEEDLES AND THREADS CAN'T BE MUCH HELP TO THE ENEMY... OR CAN THEY?

ALONE IN HIS ROOM, THE SPY DREW THE THREAD OVER A HOT LIGHT BULB, AND TINY DOTS OF INVISIBLE INK APPEARED ALONG IT. TURN THE PAGE TO SEE HOW TO USE A DOT CODE. ➤➤

Dot code messages

Dear Grandma
How are you? It is very nice in the country. Arthur got chased by a ~~co~~ cow today. Albert got chased by a lot of bees. I am having a good time in the country.   Love
                    Frances
    P.S. Here is Albert being chased by the bees.

| A | B | C | D | E | F | G | H | I | J | K | L | M | N | O | P | Q | R | S | T | U | V | W | X | Y | Z |

This letter is really a secret spy message. Each bee in the picture stands for one letter of the message. To find the message, first trace the code strip below the picture. Hold the strip with its end right at the edge of the picture and slide it slowly down the page to match each bee with a letter. (The top bee stands for H.)

In this code each letter is made by dotting a piece of paper or a piece of string in a special place.
A string message is easy to hide – you could even tie it round a parcel. And the dots on a piece of paper can be disguised inside a picture.

To encode a message you need a paper strip carefully printed with the alphabet. To decode the message, your contact needs a strip just like yours. For extra secrecy use a keyword to scramble the letters of the alphabet.

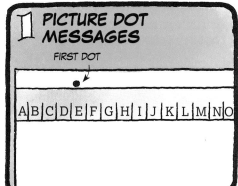

1 PICTURE DOT MESSAGES
FIRST DOT

| A | B | C | D | E | F | G | H | I | J | K | L | M | N | O |

On this code strip you needn't leave space at the start. Hold the strip near the top of a piece of paper. Put a dot over the first letter of the message.

1 DISGUISING THE DOTS

You can disguise the dot message as a picture. For example, you could turn the dots into birds, like this.

1 STRING DOT MESSAGES

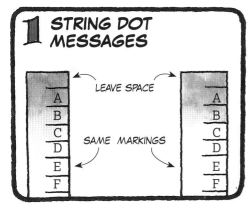

Mark a strip of paper into 27 spaces about 1cm (½in) wide. Tell your contact to mark his or her strip the same way. Leave a space and write the alphabet as shown.

2

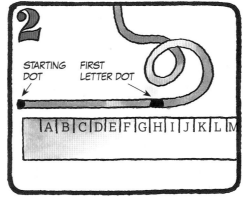

Make a starting dot at the end of a piece of string. Hold the string along the strip like this and dot it with ink at the first letter of the message.

3

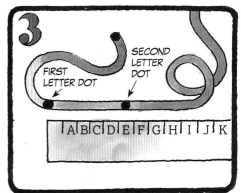

Move the first dot to the starting point and make a second dot at the second letter of the message. Move each dot to the start before you make the next dot.

2

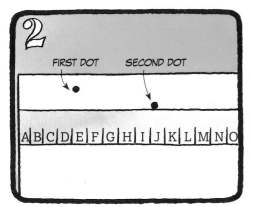

Move the strip down slightly and put a second dot over the second letter of the message. Continue to move the strip down to make each new dot.

3

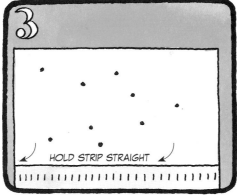

To decode the message your contact moves their strip down the page and 'reads' each dot. They must hold the strip very straight, with its end at the paper edge.

2

Or the dots could become points on a jagged line, to look like part of a chart.

3

You could even disguise the message as a board game. The snake's eyes here are the same dots.

KEYWORD SCRAMBLER

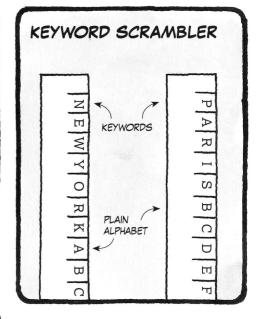

Suppose a lot of people know how to use the ordinary code strip. To keep them from reading your messages, make a special strip that only you and your contact know about. Choose a word with all-different letters, such as those above. This will be your keyword. Write the letters of this word in the first spaces of the code strip. Then write in the alphabet as before, skipping the letters you have already used.

Knot messages

Black Hat is being held prisoner by the QZ Spy Ring. He has been shut in a room with only a bed, chair and a small, barred window. All of his spy equipment has been taken from him. There is just one way to get a message to the outside world – he tears his bed sheet into long, thin strips, knots the strips and dangles a Morse code knot message out of the window.

Read on to learn how to send your own Morse knot messages.

MORSE CODE

In Morse code, just two signals – long and short – are used to make all the different letters of the alphabet. The short signal is called a dot (●) and the long signal is called a dash (–). There is a sample of Morse code on the right below and the whole Morse alphabet is shown on page 44.

MORSE KNOT MESSAGES

Use the Morse alphabet to encode your message in dots and dashes. Then make knots in a long piece of string to stand for the dots and dashes. Use a thumb knot for a dot and a figure of eight knot for a dash. On the right you will see how to make both knots.

Always begin your message with a thumb knot right at the end of the string. This will show your contact where to start when he or she decodes the message. (Black Hat's message does not have a starting knot because it does not matter whether you read it forwards or backwards.) Leave a big space between letters and a bigger space between words.

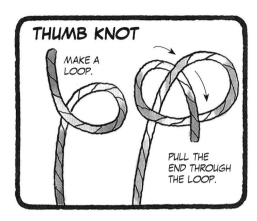

THUMB KNOT

MAKE A LOOP.

PULL THE END THROUGH THE LOOP.

Make a loop of string. Pull one end of the string through the loop. You've probably made this knot often.

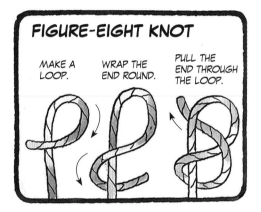

FIGURE-EIGHT KNOT

MAKE A LOOP.

WRAP THE END ROUND.

PULL THE END THROUGH THE LOOP.

Make a loop of string. Wrap the end of the string once around the straight piece. Then pull it through the loop.

MORSE KNOTS

THIS SAYS F.

THIS SAYS F.

This picture shows the letter F in the ordinary Morse code and in knots. The dots are made by little thumb knots and the dash is made by the bigger figure of eight knot.

Picture messages

A Morse code message can be hidden in a picture. Notice that in this picture there is a row of small and large birds and a row of short and tall flowers. Each of these rows spells the name of a car, in Morse. For example the first flower stem has three short flowers and then a tall flower. This group makes V (●●●–) in Morse. The flowers on each stem stand for one letter. The whole row makes a word. Find the groups of dots and dashes in each row and then decode with the Morse alphabet on page 44.

There is a third word somewhere in the picture – can you find it?

To make a Morse picture message, first encode your message in dots and dashes. Then for each word draw a row of short and tall things or small and large things to stand for the dots and dashes. You will find some ideas on the right. The drawings that make a letter should be in a group and the groups that make a word should be in a row. Start the message at the top of the page and work from left to right as in a written message.

Show dots and dashes by small and large things in a row, or by short and tall things in a row. For example, here are three ways to make the letter R (●–●).

31

Quick disguises

These quick disguises can help you fool your enemy. If your enemy is following at a distance, he or she will keep track of you by watching for something special about the way that you look. Start out with a disguise that will catch his or her eye. Wear a bright scarf or a sling or use a special walk (see below). Then go into a building or duck into a doorway and come out without it. Your enemy will be left wondering where you've gone.

Spy language:
Following is known as 'shadowing' or 'tailing'. The person who does it is a 'tail' or a 'shadow'.

CHANGE YOUR WALK

A good spy trick is to pretend you have a stiff leg or a limp. But you might forget your stiff leg, or start limping on the wrong foot.

Here are some ways to make sure that you remember:
1   To make yourself limp, put a small stone in one shoe.
2   For a stiff leg, put a ruler at the back of one knee and tie it on with a scarf. Then you won't be able to bend it. Wear something long to hide the ruler.

ARM IN SLING

You will need a helper to put your arm in a sling. Use a big scarf or a piece of cloth folded like this. Hold your arm across it and put a corner around your neck. Lift the bottom corner and knot it to the piece around your neck. Then pin the side cover over your elbow, as shown.

ONE-ARMED SPY

ARM INSIDE COAT

SLEEVE IN POCKET

Wear your coat like this to look as though you only have one arm. Put one arm into a sleeve. Tuck the other sleeve into a pocket. Button the coat with one arm inside.

TWO-WAY SCARF

KNOT THREAD

TAKE OUT PINS AFTER STITCHING.

To make a quick-change scarf you will need two scarves the same size and shape but different shades or patterns. Pin them together like this and stitch around all four sides.

CHANGE YOUR SHAPE

1

PUT ON TOWEL.

WITH DISGUISE

WITHOUT DISGUISE

HAT AND TOWEL IN BAG

To raise your shoulders, lay a small towel behind your neck, like this. Then put a coat on over it. This will help you look like an older person with muscular shoulders. To change your back view even more, wear a hat or scarf as well. Take a folded plastic bag in your pocket. Later you can carry the hat and towel in the bag.

2

To make yourself look fatter, tie a small cushion around your middle. Button a coat on over it, or wear a very big sweater.

Change your looks

If your enemy knows you and is watching for you, try these tricks.

WHITE HAIR

Put talcum powder on your hair and eyebrows to whiten them. If you are fair they will go white and if you are dark they will go grey. Do just the front if you wear a hat.

HAIR COMBED WRONG WAY

Comb your hair a different way. Slick it back or part it in a different place. If you have a fringe, comb it to the side.

CHANGED EYEBROWS

Cover your eyebrows by rubbing bits of damp, soft soap into them. It might help to use face powder over the soap. Then draw new eyebrows with a black crayon.

FACE COLOURS

To make your face paler, rub some talcum powder on it. Rub it in gently and don't use too much. Use cocoa powder to make your face look browner.

MISSING TOOTH

From a distance, a blacked-out tooth looks like a gap. First wipe the tooth dry. Then rub black crayon over it.

5 O'CLOCK SHADOW

Mix daubs of blue and black paint with some face cream. Rub a little on your face like this, to look as though you need a shave.

LUMPY FACE

Put small wads of cotton wool between your teeth and cheeks. Stick in lots to make fat cheeks. To make lumpy jowls just put them next to your lower teeth.

WRINKLE LINES

Draw wrinkle lines with a soft pencil, like a pencil marked 3B or 4B. Smile very hard, then wrinkle your forehead to see where the lines should go.

Disguises to make

1 FALSE BEARD

Knot the ends of a piece of string around your ears. Add a small piece as shown. Glue it to a big piece of cotton wool. Pinch the cotton wool round the string.

2

PULL OUT HAIRS

When the beard is quite dry, dip it in a bowl of watery paint to colour it. Gently pull the wet cotton wool to make it hairy. Hang it to dry for a day or two.

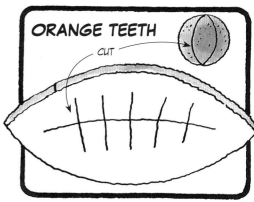

ORANGE TEETH

CUT

Cut and peel off a piece of orange skin and make cuts in it, as shown. Wear it between your lips and real teeth, with the white side out.

For the bald head you will need:

- a balloon and some string
- papier mâché and coloured wool
- scissors and glue

For the beard you will need:

- thick string and strong glue
- a roll of cotton wool
- scissors and poster paint

For the false nose you will need:

- plasticine and papier mâché
- poster paint

For the spectacles you will need:

- scissors and sticky tape
- thin cardboard and poster paint

MAKING PAPIER MÂCHÉ

Soak small pieces of newspaper in paste. Use wallpaper paste or make a thick mixture of flour and water. Build up the papier mâché shape with layers of soaked paper. Drying time is two or three days.

1 BALD HEAD WIG

Blow up a balloon until it is about the size of your head and tie the opening shut. Cover it with papier mâché, as shown. Use about three layers.

2

When the papier mâché is dry, pop the balloon with the point of your scissors. Trim the edge of the shape to look like this.

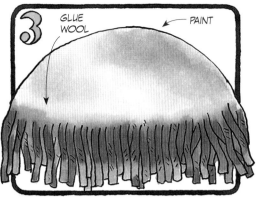

3

GLUE WOOL   PAINT

Paint the shape in colours that match your face. Then cut some wool into short pieces. Glue them round the edge of the bald head to look like hair.

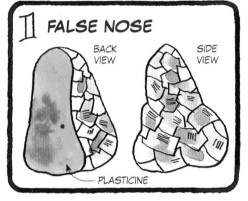

1 FALSE NOSE

BACK VIEW   SIDE VIEW

PLASTICINE

Make a nose shape with plasticine. Make it at least as big as your own nose and a different shape. Cover it with papier mâché, as shown. Use about three layers.

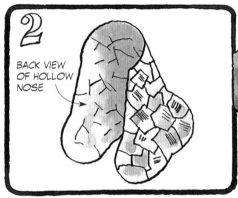

2

BACK VIEW OF HOLLOW NOSE

When the shape is dry, prod out the plasticine with a pencil. Paint the shape to match your face. Trim it with scissors to fit your nose. A small one will stay on by itself.

3

TAPE

To make a big nose stay on, fasten it with sticky tape to a pair of spectacles, like this. Run the tape from the front of the nose over the specs and down the inside.

FALSE SPECTACLES

NOSE PIECE

FOLD

TRACE THIS PATTERN WITH A PENCIL.

TAPE ON CARD

1

Copy this shape onto a folded piece of light card. Make sure the nose piece is on the fold.

2

Cut out the spaces for the glass and then cut the outside shape. Cut the pattern side first. Then you can draw round it to make the pattern for the other side.

3

Paint the specs with poster paint. Then straighten the nose piece by taping a matching bit of cardboard to it. Wind sticky tape round both pieces of cardboard.

Spotting clues

A spy must be very good at spotting clues. He or she has to get information from little signs and marks that other people would not notice. This page shows how to get information from footprints and from car and cycle tracks. This can be very useful if you lose sight of someone you are following. Sometimes the person you are following may disguise themselves. Watch out for clues that can help you see through the disguise. Try the spy test below to see how good you are at spotting this kind of clue.

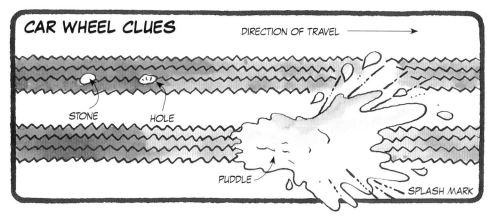

CAR WHEEL CLUES

DIRECTION OF TRAVEL →

STONE

HOLE

PUDDLE

SPLASH MARK

A stone hit by a car wheel is pressed down to make a hole and then kicked back. The marks left in the road show the direction in which the car was going.

When a wheel hits a puddle it splashes the oil or water forwards. Look for the splash mark to work out which way the wheel was going.

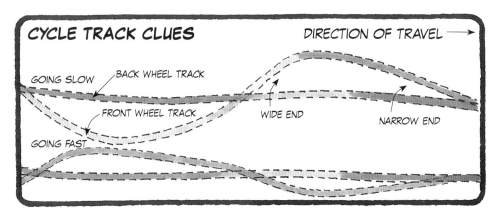

CYCLE TRACK CLUES

DIRECTION OF TRAVEL →

GOING SLOW

BACK WHEEL TRACK

FRONT WHEEL TRACK

WIDE END

NARROW END

GOING FAST

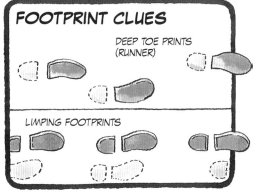

FOOTPRINT CLUES

DEEP TOE PRINTS (RUNNER)

LIMPING FOOTPRINTS

The front wheel of a cycle makes a loopy track, because the cyclist has to keep his or her balance. The wheels turn less when going fast and make smaller loops.

After turning the wheel, the cyclist straightens it, so the loops are always wider at one end than the other. The narrow end points out where he or she is heading.

If the person you are trailing is running, look for a deep toe print and light heel print. If they are limping, look for a deep footprint and then a light footprint.

SPY TEST

SPY Z KNOWS MANY DISGUISE TRICKS. BUT HE FORGETS TO HIDE ONE CLUE. READ ON AND SEE IF YOU CAN SPOT IT.

BLACK HAT HAS JUST SPOTTED SPY Z NEAR THE PALM HOTEL.

AS SPY Z ENTERS THE HOTEL AND CALLS THE ELEVATOR, BLACK HAT IS WATCHING. NOW IS HIS CHANCE TO SEE WHERE Z HIDES OUT.

WHEN SPY Z ENTERS THE ELEVATOR BLACK HAT RUNS UPSTAIRS...

SLAM!

Trapping spies

Suppose you think that your enemy is getting into your secret hiding places. Set up one of the spy traps on this page and the intruder will be tricked into making noise or leaving a clue that shows someone has been there. Door Trap No. 2 is particularly useful. Made with flour, it leaves a mark on anyone who goes through the door.

You can make another good noise trap by sprinkling sugar on the floor. But people in socks or soft soles can avoid this trap.

HALLWAY TRAP

Tape a thin black thread from wall to wall, like this. Anyone who walks past this spot will make the thread fall down.

DESK TRAP

CLUE MARK

Spread some papers in a careless-looking way. Draw a tiny line that runs across two of them, like this. The smallest movement of the papers will break the line.

DOOR TRAP NO.1

GLUED HAIR
(GLUE IT LOW DOWN OR HIGH UP.)

Glue a hair across the opening crack, like this. Check later – if someone has gone through the door, the hair will come unglued. Use the same trap on a drawer.

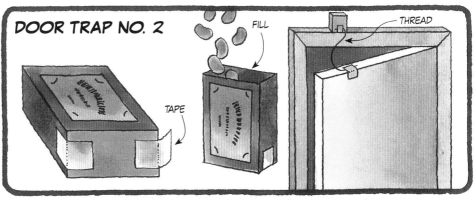

DOOR TRAP NO. 2

TAPE

FILL

THREAD

Find a very small cardboard box. Fill it with beans (for a noise trap) or with flour (for a marking trap).

Tape one end of a thread to the box and prop it on a door frame. Tape the thread to the door, like this, and close the door. When someone opens it, the box will fall.

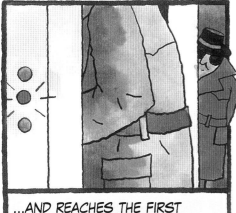

...AND REACHES THE FIRST FLOOR LANDING JUST IN TIME TO SEE A SECOND PERSON ENTER THE ELEVATOR.

ON THE NEXT FLOOR, TWO MEN GET OUT. THIS IS THE TOP FLOOR - ONE OF THEM MUST BE SPY 2 IN DISGUISE.

BLACK HAT FOLLOWS THE TWO MEN DOWN THE HALL. AS THEY TAKE OUT THEIR KEYS HE SEES THE CLUE THAT HE'S BEEN WAITING FOR. DO YOU? (SEE PAGE 46 TO FIND THE ANSWER.)

Secret telephone messages

BLACK HAT PICKS UP THE TELEPHONE AND SAYS...

ZABI DAKIDO KUKADA BUKON OZO BUBIDU KOBA BI BAGU-BE

The code spoken by Black Hat is made by using the alphabet box on the next page. Each plain letter is replaced by two of the code letters in the frame. The code can be spoken because one of the two letters is always a vowel (a, e, i, o or u). Your contact should write down the code message as he or she hears it and decode it later.

Remember – be sure that you and your contact agree on how to say the vowels, or he or she may write down the wrong letter.

THE ENEMY, LISTENING, IS BEWILDERED...

1 ENCODE YOUR MESSAGE

H E L P

(DOUBLE SPACE BELOW FOR WRITING CODE)

Print the plain message neatly. Leave space between each letter and between each line of letters.

2

H E L P

DO ZI NO GU

Replace each plain letter with the code letter on its row and the code letter on its column. Use strips of paper to line them up.

1 EXTRA SECURITY

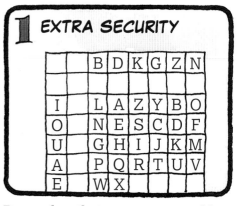

	B	D	K	G	Z	N
I	L	A	Z	Y	B	O
O	N	E	S	C	D	F
U	G	H	I	J	K	M
A	P	Q	R	T	U	V
E	W	X				

Remember that you can scramble the alphabet by starting with a keyword (a word with all different letters). Then add the rest of the letters.

1 DISGUISE YOUR VOICE

To change your voice on the telephone, hold your mouth in a funny shape or gently bite down on a pencil while you speak.

2

Now purse your lips as though you were going to whistle. Hold that shape while you speak and see what happens to your voice.

3

Now try a few more experiments. Try to speak while smiling very hard, as shown, or frowning.

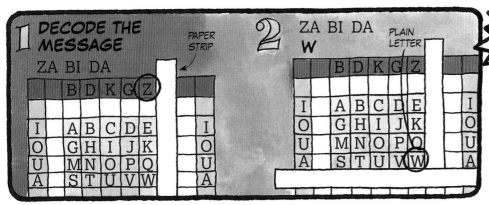

1 DECODE THE MESSAGE

ZA BI DA — PAPER STRIP

	B	D	K	G	Z
I	A	B	C	D	E
O	G	H	I	J	K
U	M	N	O	P	Q
A	S	T	U	V	W

Write out Black Hat's message in pairs of letters. The first code letter is in one of the red squares that mark the columns. Mark the column with a strip of paper.

2 ZA BI DA W — PLAIN LETTER

	B	D	K	G	Z
I	A	B	C	D	E
O	G	H	I	J	K
U	M	N	O	P	Q
A	S	T	U	V	W

You will find the second code letter in one of the blue squares that mark rows. Mark the row with a paper strip. The plain letter is where the two strips of paper meet.

SEVERAL MINUTES LATER COMES THE ANSWER...

KO ZODUZIZA KODA DADOZI BUKONOZO KOBA BAKUKANU

2 CHANGEABLE LETTERS

	F	G	L	S	T	N
I	A	B	C	D	E	F
O	G	H	I	J	K	L
U	M	N	O	P	Q	R
A	S	T	U	V	W	X
E	Y	Z				

Or use different code letters to mark the columns. You can use any letters except vowels (the letters that mark the rows).

4

Now try holding your nose while you practise the methods shown. You will find that your voice is completely different.

ALPHABET BOX

CODE LETTERS →

	B	D	K	G	Z	N	
I	A	B	C	D	E	F	I
O	G	H	I	J	K	L	O
U	M	N	O	P	Q	R	U
A	S	T	U	V	W	X	A
E	Y	Z					E
	B	D	K	G	Z	N	

Make the code for each plain letter with one letter from a red square and one letter from a blue square.

The picture shows how to encode the letter K. It doesn't matter whether you say OZ or ZO.

Silent signals

If you and your contact can see each other but cannot speak or get close enough to pass a message, signal with the silent alphabet shown on the page on the right. Or blink the Morse code as shown below and on page 44. In a crowded room or busy street you and your contact can send quick messages or warnings with silent hand and leg signals.

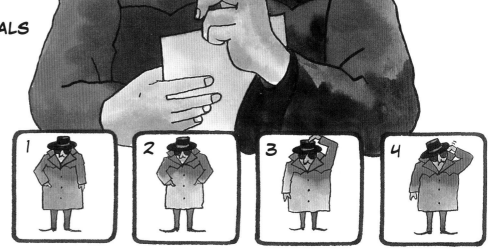

SILENT HAND AND LEG SIGNALS

1 Hand in pocket – yes.

2 Hands in pockets – no.

3 Scratching head – can you meet me at the hiding place?

4 Scratching back of neck – be careful: you're being watched.

5 Crossing legs – leave your message at the 'drop'.

6 Both hands behind back – I can't pass the message now.

7 Scratching ear – I will telephone you later.

8 On one leg with hand in pocket – I'm going home.

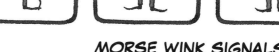

MORSE BLINK SIGNALS

Blink for a count of one to make a dot and blink for a count of three to make a dash. A stare means the end of a word or message.

MORSE WINK SIGNALS

Wink to make a dot and blink to make a dash. A stare means the end of a word or message.

Silent alphabet

On this page you can see how to make the letters of the alphabet with your hands. The pictures show how the hand signals should look to your contact. Don't try this in front of a mirror – the reflected signals will be the wrong way around. You and your contact could try doing the signals together to get them right.

At the bottom of the page you'll find quick signs to answer questions or to show whether or not you understand.

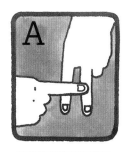 A
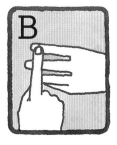 B
 C
 D

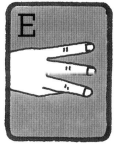 E
 F
 G
 H

 I
 J
 K
 L
 M
 N

 O
 P
 Q
 R
 S
 T

 U
 V
 W
 X
 Y
 Z

 QUICK SIGNS
 YES
 NO
 UNDERSTOOD
 NOT UNDERSTOOD
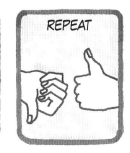 REPEAT

Semaphore signals

If you and your contact can see each other but are too far away to talk, you can send messages in semaphore. In this code you make the letters of the alphabet by standing with your arms held in the positions shown on the opposite page. Hold your arms very straight to make a good clear signal. If you hold out flags the signal can be seen from very far away.

Use the extra signals shown below to make sure your contact is ready to receive your message and understands it.

MAKING SIGNALS

THIS IS THE SIGNAL FOR 'A'.

THIS IS JUST A BENT ARM – NOT A SIGNAL.

Hold your arm straight to make the signal clearly. Don't let it bend or wobble.

Practise with your contact to make sure your signals can be easily understood.

1 SENDER'S SIGNALS

Wave your arms back and forth between these two positions to say 'I am about to send a message.' Wait for the 'ready' signal before you start the message.

2

Hold both arms straight out to mean 'end of word'. Drop your arms and repeat the signal to mean 'end of the message'.

3 CROSS UNCROSS

Cross and uncross your arms like this when you've made a mistake. Then send the whole word again.

1 RECEIVER'S SIGNALS

Hold your left arm like this to signal 'ready'. At the end of a word or message, make the same signal to say 'understood'.

2 CROSS UNCROSS

Cross and uncross your arms like this to say 'not ready' or to say 'not understood'.

HOLDING FLAGS

RIGHT WRONG

If your contact is very far away you can hold out flags to make the signal clearer. Hold them in a straight line from your arm.

Semaphore alphabet

On this page you can see Black Hat making each letter of the alphabet as a semaphore signal.

On the left of each picture of Black Hat you can see how to write the signal he is making.

43

Morse code

Morse is a particularly useful code because it can be sent in so many different ways. You can signal it with a buzzer or a whistle or by flashing a light on a dark night. Morse can also be tapped out or blinked with your eyes. This page shows the Morse code alphabet.

In this code (●) stands for a short signal and a dash (–) stands for a long signal. To time the signals correctly, remember that a dash is always three times as long as a dot. For example, you should flash your light for a count of one to make a dot and for a count of three to make a dash.

Don't run the letters or words together. Between two letters, wait for a count of three. Between two words, wait for a count of five. Use the extra signals shown below to make sure that your contact is ready to receive your message and that he or she understands it.

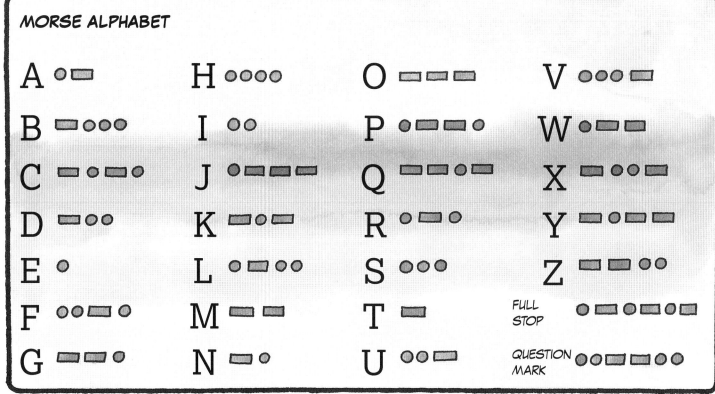

MORSE ALPHABET

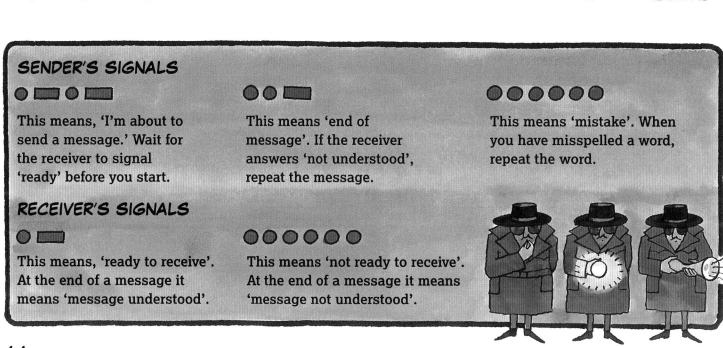

SENDER'S SIGNALS

This means, 'I'm about to send a message.' Wait for the receiver to signal 'ready' before you start.

This means 'end of message'. If the receiver answers 'not understood', repeat the message.

This means 'mistake'. When you have misspelled a word, repeat the word.

RECEIVER'S SIGNALS

This means, 'ready to receive'. At the end of a message it means 'message understood'.

This means 'not ready to receive'. At the end of a message it means 'message not understood'.

Quick signal code

This is a special code to use for signalling if you don't have time to learn the whole Morse alphabet. With this code you can send any message with just six signals.

The code is made with an alphabet box. Each plain letter is replaced by the two code letters that line up with it in the frame of the box. There are six different code letters in the frame. They are written in capitals at the side and in small letters at the top of the box. The code pair should start with a capital. For example, the code pair used for R is Oi.

Learn the Morse or semaphore signals for the six letters used. Encode the message before you start signalling. Your contact should write down the code message as he or she receives it and decode it later.

To make the code more secret, start the plain alphabet with a keyword, like 'crazy'. Then add the other letters of the alphabet.

TELEPHONE MESSAGES

You can read off the code pairs like this. Say 'adle' for A, 'eedle' for E, 'idle' for I, 'odle' for O, 'yewdle' for U, and 'wydle' for Y.

If you turn the coded message into Morse you can read it out by saying 'iddy' for a dot and 'umpty' for a dash. Remember to wait for a count of three between two letters. Between two words, wait for a count of five.

ALPHABET BOX

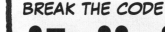

CODE LETTERS	e	a	i	o	u
E	A	B	C	D	E
A	F	G	H	I	J
I	K	L	M	N	O
O	P	Q	R	S	T
U	U	V	W	X	Y
Y	Z				

Replace each plain letter with the capital letter on its row and the small letter on its column.

Always start with a capital. For example, the code pair for R is Oi.

BREAK THE CODE

HERE IS A MESSAGE BLACK HAT HAS JUST ENCODED, READY FOR SIGNALLING. CAN YOU BREAK THE CODE?

REMEMBER - THE FIRST LETTER OF EACH CODE PAIR COMES FROM THE SIDE OF THE BOX.

Answers

Pages 2–3:
There are four secret passwords on these pages. They are 'Washington', 'Madrid', 'Paris' and 'Bologna'. Can you find them? (Use pig-pen and a code wheel.)

Pages 6–7:
The clue to the spy post office trail is 'Volkswagen'.

Page 11:
The window message says, 'Warn all to leave town at once.'

Pages 12–13:
Here is what the quick code messages say:
At start – 'Meet girl in red hat at clock tower.'
At clock tower – 'Talk about roses to flower seller at fountain.'
At fountain – 'Ask man at statue for light for cigar.'
At statue – 'Stand near church door till old man arrives.'
At church – 'Wait under tree for lady with white cat.'

At tree – 'Man with arm in sling waits on bridge.'
At bridge – 'Buy a dictionary at the book stall and open at page 10.'
At book stall – 'Master spy was the one you last met.'

Page 14:
The music code message says, 'We leave tonight.' The pig-pen code message says, 'Send new code immediately.' The railfence code says, 'Change the password.'

Page 16:
The message in Code T says, 'Watch out for stranger with black hat.'

Page 18:
The code grille message says, 'Light in east top window means all is lost.'

Page 26:
The password between the lines is 'cola'.

Page 28:
The message made by the bees is 'Help is on the way.'

Page 30:
The message made by the knots is 'S.O.S.'

Page 31:
In the picture message the sitting birds spell out 'VW'. The flowers spell out 'Volvo'. The fence posts spell out 'Buick'.

Pages 36–37:
The first few pictures show that the spy is left-handed. The left-handed man in the last picture is the spy, wearing a disguise.

Pages 38–39:
Black Hat is saying, 'Watch out – milkman is a spy.' His contact answers, 'I knew it – the milk is sour.'

Page 45:
The coded Morse message says, 'Happy spying.'

Spy language

bug – a very small microphone hidden in a room so that people talking can be overheard by the enemy.

contact – a spy friend, particularly one you meet by arrangement.

courier – a spy who carried secret messages or who carries orders from master spy to spy.

dead – 'Victor is dead' means 'Victor has been caught by the enemy.'

dead-letter box – hiding place for secret messages.

drop – hiding place for secret messages.

ill – 'Victor is ill' means, 'Victor is being watched by the enemy.'

letter-box – a person who holds secret messages for spies to pick up.

master spy – head of a spy ring.

plain language – a message in plain language when it has not been encoded.

shadow – someone who is following or 'shadowing' another person.

spy ring – a group of spies who work together. The master spy gives the orders, the couriers carry the orders to the spies, and the spies carry out the orders.

tail – someone who is following or 'tailing' another person.

Index